How to Write a Resume

Learn How to Craft Professional Resume to Find Your Dream Job Easily (cover letters, resume templates, sample resumes)

Richard Bolles

Copyright © 2014 Richard Bolles

All rights reserved.

ISBN-13: 978-1500802325

ISBN-10: 1500802328

2

All rights reserved. This book may not be reproduced, transmitted, or stored in whole or in part by any means, including graphic, electronic, or mechanical without the express written consent of the author except in the case of brief quotations embodied in critical articles and reviews.

Contents

Introduction

1. **What is a Resume**

2. **Things to Keep in Mind**

3. **Parts of the Resume** (Heading, Objective Statement, Job Experience, Education, Skills and Qualifications, Awards and Achievements, References)

4. **The Reference Sheet**

5. **Cover Letters**

6. **Making Sure You are Ready**

7. **Resume Sample**

8. **Cover Letter Samples**

9. **Reference Sheet Samples**

10. **The Interview**

Conclusion

DETROIT PUBLIC LIBRARY
TEEN CENTER
5201 WOODWARD AVE.
DETROIT MI 48202

Introduction

Everyone in the business world knows that having a good, strong resume can mean the difference between getting a job and not getting a job. You will need to have a resume that is crafted professionally and that will reflect you, your job abilities, and your experience.

Having a good looking resume is so important when you are searching for a job that it should be your number one priority. There are all sorts of ways you can go about crafting a resume that works, but there is no magic formula for a resume that will work all the time.

The choice really is up to you how you put together a resume, but there are certain nuances that you will need to be included in your resume that every employer looks for.

It is not difficult to put together a resume that works, but it is important that you not overlook what makes your resume most effective. This one or two page document speaks about you, your abilities, your experience, your education, and your accomplishments.

It is the first thing that a potential employer will see before he or she meets you, so you want it to really be compelling and make them want to pick up the phone and call you for an interview!

There are all sorts of schools of thought regarding how a resume should look, what information it should contain, and how to put it together. However, most business people agree that when they look at a resume of a potential employee, they want the resume to be concise, to the point, and easy to read.

Whichever school of thought you, as a job seeker, subscribe to, you will still want your resume to be what a potential employer wants to see. That is why you will want as much information about resumes as possible so you can have something that you can be proud to send out as an introduction to you and what you can do for a company.

What we will do inside the pages of this book is show you a few different ways to craft a resume. We will cover the important parts of this document and show you ways to make your resume a work of art! We will also give you some tips and tricks to get your resume noticed over another applicant.

While we're at it, we'll also give you some advice about the job interview and what you can do to land that job. Finding the job of your dreams isn't always as simple as just filling out a job application and then waiting for a call. It takes some aggression on your part and the right tools. We think we can help!

1

What is a Resume

The resume is a selling tool that outlines your skills and experiences so an employer can see, at a glance, how you can contribute to the employer's workplace. Your resume has to sell you in short order.

While you may have all the requirements for a particular position, your resume is a failure if the employer does not instantly come to the conclusion that you "have what it takes."

The first hurdle your resume has to pass--whether it ends up in the "consider file" or the "reject file"--may take less than thirty seconds.

The most effective resumes are clearly focused on a specific job title and address the employer's stated requirements for the position. The more you know about the duties and skills required for the job--and organize your resume around these points--the more effective the resume.

You will need information to write a good resume. Not just information about jobs you've held in the past but also information to select the most relevant accomplishments, skills and experience for THIS position. The more you know about the employer and the position, the more you can tailor your resume to fit the job.

Some people think of a resume as their "life on a page," but how could anyone put everything important about herself on a single piece of paper (or two)? Actually, resumes are much more specific, including only relevant information about you for specific employers.

Like a life, however, a resume is always growing and changing. As your career goals shift or the job market changes--as you grow personally and professionally--chances are you will need to re-write your resume or at least create new versions. Writing a resume is a lifelong process.

How do you know what in your life--past, present, and future--is most relevant to prospective employers? How do you select which information to include? The quick answer to both these questions is "it depends." It depends on your individual career goals as well as on the professional goals of the companies hiring in your area or field of interest.

In the end, only you, through research, planning, questioning and self-reflection, can determine the shape and content of your resume, but the strategies below along with those on the job search can help you ask the right questions and begin exploring your options.

Depending on whom you ask, a resume may be viewed as the single most important vehicle to securing your next job, or it may be viewed as an unnecessary nuisance.

In both cases, this is incorrect. A resume is a professional introduction meant to encourage a one-on-one interview situation - the opportunity for communication that can lead to a job offer.

It is a rare candidate who is hired by his or her resume alone. It is just as rare to be offered an interview without one.

A resume is often the first line of contact. It establishes a first impression of a potential job candidate's skills, background and hiring value. If written well, this impression can be a positive one, offering the reader a sense of the candidate's "fit" for the position and company being targeted.

If written really well, it may convince the reader that the job candidate is ideally suited for the job. When coupled with an effective cover letter, the resume can be a very strong marketing tool.

Preparing a resume may be seen as a nuisance, but having a well-constructed, well-designed resume is an important part of your job search. Consider that for each available job opening there may be as many as 100 to 1000 resumes submitted.

If your resume fails to adequately and accurately convey your hiring value (for the specific position), fails to establish your hiring value over competing candidates, or is difficult to follow, your ability to compete against those 100 to 1000 professionals vying for the same position your are will be greatly diminished.

If your resume secures an interview, it has done its job. If it sets you ahead of the competition in the mind of your interviewer, then it has given you a distinct advantage, and has gone beyond its job.

A great resume does what all good marketing pieces do: it sells the "consumer" (the potential employer or hiring manager) on the "product" (you).

Like it or not, the job of looking for employment is a job in sales and marketing. The product you are "selling" is you, and the "customer," who has unique needs and interests, needs to be sold on the fact that you have what it takes to get the job done and to meet the needs of the position.

He or she is going to want to know how you are going to solve his or her problems, and he or she is going to give your resume about 15 seconds, or less, to sell this. 15 seconds is the average time a hiring manager will allot to a new resume - before giving it a potential "yes" or "no" response.

The resume will not get you the job (well, it has happened, but it is extremely rare), but it can certainly secure your chances of being seen and interviewed, just as it can cause you to be passed over in favor of a candidate who offers a better presentation.

As with any type of marketing campaign, use your resume as one tool in your search. Continue to network, improve your interviewing skills, and use every avenue available to you to better your chances and opportunities.

And, after you have secured that next position, do this all over again. Always be prepared for the next opportunity. Keep your resume up-to-date and stay career fit.

So, essentially, a resume is you in short form on paper. That is why having a good looking, easy to read resume is so important. Let's look at a few suggestions about your resume from the professionals.

2

Things to Keep in Mind

In preparing your resume, the more you know about the position you are targeting, the better. If you know the company's missions and goals, if you understand the needs of the position, if you recognize the company's "concerns," and if you know who comprises the company's competition, you will be prepared.

AND you (and your unique skills and experience) can meet the needs of all the above (you have accurately assessed your own value to those who have employed you in the past), you will have the material necessary to create an effective marketing piece.

As in any type of marketing material, it is important to present the information so that it captures your customer's interest quickly. Your goal is to encourage the reader to stay with your document as long as possible. Your chance for a more detailed reading increases when you give the reader that information which he or she most wants to secure, early in the document.

One of the best ways to accomplish this is to create a Summary Section at the beginning of your resume. A Summary Section highlights for your reader those personal and professional skills you possess that allow you to excel in your chosen field and position.

Items and skills of greatest importance (from your readers' viewpoint) should be listed in priority, supporting an impression of both "fit" and potential success. In addition, these should be aspects of your background that set you apart from your competing candidates, particularly candidates with skill sets similar to your own.

You are, in effect, showing your reader how you will solve their problems - better than the competition - and why interviewing you will be a worthwhile expenditure of their time.

You are not writing your resume in order to put your career autobiography out there for posterity. This is not about you - seriously. It is about how you can meet the needs of your reader - in this particular position at this particular company. It is all about them.

During the interview is when your first opportunity for negotiation takes place and you get to discuss what you get out of the deal. But right now, the only person who matters is your reader. They hold all the marbles.

When writing your resume, keep in mind your specific reader. Listing information that will be of no value to the position or company being targeted is just a waste of time.

Check for redundancy in your statements. If the positions you have held are similar, then repeating the same functions in detail throughout your document is unnecessary (heard it, got it). However, do not short-change yourself on your accomplishments.

Your potential employer is most interested in seeing how hiring you will benefit him/her and the company. If you are dealing with a hiring manager or human resource director, you can bet he or she has a lot resting on the fact that, if you are hired, they found the right person for the job.

It is expensive to hire, train, and let someone go - and it is their job to make sure this does not happen. All parties involved want to know they are making the right decision, and it is your job to assure them that they are.

The most effective way to do this is by identifying how you have benefited employers in the past. Take credit for your participation and accomplishments. While looking at the aspects of your background may seem minor or of little value to you, they may be seen as a valuable asset to those looking to fill a need.

The layout of your resume is extremely important. Your resume needs to maintain a "clean" and professional appearance (remember, it is representing you!). It should allow the reader to access the information quickly. Neat margins, adequate "white space" between groupings, and indenting to highlight text, aid the ease of reference and retention of the material.

Use "bolding" and italics sparingly. Overuse of these features actually diminishes their effectiveness of promoting the material they are intended highlight.

Your contact information (how the reader can reach you) is essentially the most important information in the entire document. Make certain your name, address, phone number, and e-mail address (if included) are clearly visible and at the top of your document (from habit, this is where your reader will look for this information - do not make them search for it).

If you are including additional pages, be certain that your name is on these secondary pages. Consider including your phone number here, too, in case your sheets become separated.

The standards for resume length have changed. It used to be typical for resumes to be one-page in length, and no longer. For candidates with years of experience, having held multiple positions, or with outstanding achievements, this one-page constraint often results in a document that is unreadable, looks "squashed," or utilizes a font size so small that the reader is required to squint (no, they won't actually bother). The one-page standard no longer holds true.

Use as much space as you need to concisely, accurately, and effectively communicate your skills, history, achievements, and accomplishments - as these relate to the position and company being targeted.

A two-page document, if presented well, will not diminish the effectiveness of your marketing strategy - as long as the information you provide is relevant and valuable to your reader's goals and interests.

A three-page resume is requiring much of your reader's time (and patience), and may not be as effective as a more concise presentation. In academic fields and European markets, it may be necessary to go over two pages in length, but only provide this much information if you absolutely cannot present your history and achievements in less.

If you are certain your reader will agree with you, they will not mind reading a resume over three pages. An overly long presentation may leave your reader wondering if you can be concise in anything you do.

Document in detail your most recent 10-15 years of employment and/or experience. Longer if the most recent position extended 10 years or more. Be certain to document growth in a company where multiple positions have been held, including identification of promotions and increased responsibilities.

List positions held prior to this in decreasing detail, unless a previous position more effectively documents relevant skills for the position you are currently targeting.

You want to entice you reader into wanting to meet you (the interview) to learn more. Current history and recently utilized skills will hold the most value.

Remember, you will have an opportunity to expand on the information in your resume during the interview. So, entice your reader to want to learn more, but don't forget to leave something to tell.

24

How do you put together a resume that will get attention? Let's take a look at each section one by one.

3

Parts of the Resume

Before you write, take time to do a self-assessment on paper. Outline your skills and abilities as well as your work experience and extracurricular activities. This will make it easier to prepare a thorough resume.

When you do this, be sure to write down dates, as it can be very important – especially in showing that you have a consistent work history.

Gaps in work history do not bear well with potential employers as it gives the impression that you are not reliable.

Gather together the names of the businesses you have worked for along with their address and phone number and the name of your immediate supervisor at the time. Do not include salary history on a general resume. If salary comes up, it will be during the interview or at the time you are – hopefully – offered the job.

Note special achievements and awards you have received along with the date you received them. You may also want to include a blurb about the qualifications that needed to be met in order to receive that award.

But we are getting ahead of ourselves. Let's begin with the heading of the resume.

The Heading

The heading of your resume provides basic contact information about you. That means your name, address, any telephone numbers you are available at and your e-mail address. You can arrange this information in a variety of ways. The simple way is like this:

Michelle Smith
555 My Bright Way
Yourtown, IL 54321
Home Phone: (555) 555-5555
Cell Phone: (555) 444-4444
e-mail: micsmith@yahoo.com

As you can see, the name is in larger print than the rest of the information and in bold. The rest of the contact information is in smaller print and not bolded.

Another format you can use for the heading looks like this:

Michelle Smith

555 My Bright Way * Yourtown, IL 54321 * Home Phone (555) 555-5555 * Cell Phone: (555) 444-4444 * micsmith@yahoo.com

Yet another way that you can construct the heading is like this:

Michelle Smith

555 My Bright Way

Yourtown, IL 54321

Home Phone (555) 555-5555 * Cell Phone (555) 444-4444 * micsmith@yahoo.com

The important thing to remember about the heading is that it contains your up-to-date pertinent information and highlights your name. Here are some other pointers to remember when writing the heading of your resume:

- Avoid nicknames.

- Use a permanent address. Use your parents' address, a friend's address, or the address you plan to use after graduation.
- Use a permanent telephone number and include the area code. If you have an answering machine, record a neutral greeting.
- Add your e-mail address. Many employers will find it useful. (Note: Choose an e-mail address that sounds professional.)
- Include your web site address only if the web page reflects your professional ambitions.

The next section is your objective statement.

The Objective Statement

There are two schools of thought regarding an objective statement. Some people say you shouldn't include this on a resume because that is what your cover letter is for. Other people say that stating what you want to accomplish in your career is probably the most important part of the resume.

You can choose to include an objective statement if you like, but if you do, you need to know a few things. First and foremost, this statement should be brief and concise – not more than a sentence or two. An objective tells potential employers the sort of work you're hoping to do.

Be specific about the job you want. For example: To obtain an entry-level position within a financial institution requiring strong analytical and organizational skills. Tailor your objective to each employer you target/every job you seek.

Objective statements improve your resume by helping you:

- Emphasize your main qualifications and summarize them for readers
- Inform your readers of the position(s) you are seeking and your career goals
- Establish your professional identity

To improve your chances for success, it's always a good idea to tailor your objective statement (as well as your whole resume and cover letter) to particular organizations and/or positions. This means, for example, calling a position by the name the company uses to describe it. You might even indicate the organization's name in your statement.

Strive to match your qualifications with those desired by the organization. If you are unsure what your résumé's readers will be looking for, you'll need to do some research to give your objective statement a competitive edge.

Before drafting or revising your objective statement, you will find it helpful to answer as many of the following questions as possible.

About You:

- What are your main qualifications (strengths, skills, areas of expertise)

- What positions (or range of positions) do you seek?
- What are your professional goals?
- What type of organization or work setting are you interested in?

<u>About the Company or Organization</u>:

- Which of your qualifications are most desired by your résumé's readers?
- What position titles (or range or positions) are available?
- What are some goals of the organizations that interest you?
- What types of organizations or work settings are now hiring?

The most common mistake made in writing objective statements is being too general and vague in describing either the position desired or your qualifications. For example, some objective statements read like this:

An internship allowing me to utilize my knowledge and expertise in different areas.

Such an objective statement raises more questions than it answers: What kind of internship? What knowledge? What kinds of expertise? Which areas? Be as specific as possible in your objective statement to help your readers see what you have to offer "at a glance."

To come up with an objective statement that is effective, try one of these formulas:

1. To emphasize a particular position and your relevant qualifications

    A position as a [name or type of position] allowing me to use my [qualifications]

    To utilize my [qualifications] as a [position title]

A position as a Support Specialist allowing me to use my skills in the fields of computer science and management information systems

2. To emphasize the field or type of organization you want to work in and your professional goal or your main qualifications

An opportunity to [professional goal] in a [type of organization, work environment, or field]

To enter [type of organization, work environment, or field] allowing me to use my [qualifications]

An opportunity to obtain a loan officer position, with eventual advancement to vice president for lending services, in a growth-oriented bank

To join an aircraft research team allowing me to apply my knowledge of avionics and aircraft electrical systems

3. To emphasize your professional or career goal or an organizational goal

    To [professional goal]

    An opportunity to [professional goal]

    To help children and families in troubled situations by utilizing my child protection services background

4. A specific position desired

    [position name]

    Technical writer specializing in user documentation

Some things to keep in mind when formulating your objective statement include the following:

- Integrate key words and phrases used in the job advertisement(s)
- Play with word choices to fit your strengths and your readers' expectations. You might try
    - Substituting for "use" words like "develop," "apply," or "employ," etc.
    - Replacing "allowing me" with "requiring" or "giving me the opportunity," etc.
    - Changing "enter" to "join," "pursue," "obtain," "become a member," "contribute," etc.
- Blend two or more of the above generic models or create your own!

Depending on the format of your resume, the objective section should be written in sentence format with its own heading.

The next two sections are interchangeable depending on which applies the most to the position you are applying for. If you think your job experience is more relevant to the job then list "job experience" next. If it is your education that will help most, then put that section next.

Job Experience

This is the most complex section of your resume, and it is required, although you have a great deal of freedom in the way your present your experiences. To get started on this section, make a list of your job titles and the names, dates and locations of places where you worked.

Break each job (paid or unpaid) into short, descriptive phrases or sentences that begin with action verbs. These phrases will highlight the skills you used on the job, and help the employer envision you as an active person in the workplace. Use action words to describe the work you did.

You may choose special typestyles, **bolding**, <u>underlining</u>, or placement to draw your reader's attention to the information you want to emphasize. When the company you worked for is more impressive than your job title, you may want to highlight that information.

Briefly give the employer an overview of work that has taught you skills. Include your work experience in reverse chronological order—that is, put your last job first and work backward to your first, relevant job. Include:

- Title of position,
- Name of organization
- Location of work (town, state)
- Dates of employment
- Describe your work responsibilities with emphasis on specific skills and achievements.

You should probably not go back more than your three previous jobs so that your resume doesn't get too long. However, you will want to include any job experience that is relevant to the job you are applying for to show you have experience in that field.

Depending on how you are formatting your resume, there are a couple of ways that you can put this section together. Here are a couple of ways you can try this:

April, 1998 - Present   XYZ Corporation; Anywhere, IL
Position: Sales Analyst
Duties: To monitor sales activities for 20 sales people, calculate profit/loss margins, make suggestions for improvement, hold educational seminars to insures sales are progressing as they should, prepare annual statements, formulate and implement new

procedures to improve efficiency

~~~~~~~~~~~~~~~~~~~~~~~~~~~~~~~

XYZ Corporation; Anywhere, IL

April, 1998 – Present

Position: Sales Analyst

Duties: To monitor sales activities for 20 sales people, calculate, profit/loss margins, make suggestions for improvement, hold educational seminars to insure sales is progressing as it should, prepare annual statements, formulate and implement new procedures to improve efficiency

~~~~~~~~~~~~~~~~~~~~~~~~~~~~~~~

XYZ Corporation; Anywhere, IL

April, 1998 – Present

Sales Analyst

- To monitor sales activities for 20 sales people
- Calculate, profit/loss margins
- Make suggestions for improvement

- Hold educational seminars to insure sales is progressing as it should
- Prepare annual statements
- Formulate and implement new procedures to improve efficiency

There are many, many more ways that you can layout this section and it all depend on how your whole resume is laid out. As long as you have the basic information about what company you worked for, when you worked for them, your position at the company, and your job duties, then you should be covered.

Next is the education section.

Education

This section can be set up much like the job experience section – it all really depends on what format you are choosing for your resume. This section is an important one for most students, and it is a required element of the resume. In this section, you should include:

- The name and location of your college or university
- Your degree and graduation date
- Your major(s) and minor(s)
- Grade point average (your cumulative GPA and your major GPA are optional)

Use placement of information, bold type or underlining to highlight the features you want to emphasize. It is sometimes necessary to pinpoint a feature or features that make you standout among other students.

For example, students bold their university or college if they feel like that is a distinctive feature. Others may decide to bold their type of degree.

New graduates without a lot of work experience should list their educational information first. Alumni can list it after the work experience section.

Be sure the following is included in the education section of your resume:

- Your most recent educational information is listed first.
- Include your degree (A.S., B.S., B.A., etc.)
- Your major, institution attended, and your minor/concentration.
- Add your grade point average (GPA) if it is higher than 3.0.
- Mention academic honors.

Here are two examples of education sections, with different information emphasized.

Purdue University, West Lafayette, Indiana
Bachelor of Science, May 1999
Major: Supervision; GPA 5.5/6.0

Bachelor of Science in Accounting, May 1999
Minor in Finance, GPA: 5.5/6.0 Major, 5.2/6.0 Overall
Purdue University, West Lafayette, Indiana

In your education section, you may want to include a couple of sub-groups – especially if you are a recent graduate looking for your first position. The first sub-group is "Related Course Work".

This is an optional part of your Education section, which can be quite impressive and informative for potential employers. Students seeking internships may want to list all completed major-related courses.

Graduates might list job-related courses different than those required to receive the degree (employers will already be aware of those). Include high-level courses in optional concentrations, foreign languages, computer applications or communications classes. You may choose more meaningful headings such as "Computer Applications" if you wish to emphasize particular areas.

Remember - employers and recruiters are familiar with the basic courses required in your major. Limit these sections to special courses or skills you have to offer.

Another optional sub-group in the education section is "Special Projects". This optional section may be added to point out special features of your education that are particularly interesting to employers or that may make you more qualified than others for the job you are seeking.

Students often include research, writing, or computer projects. Limit your description to the most important facts. You may expand your discussion in your application letter.

If you like, you can include any awards you received or special achievements in this section, but most resumes will have a separate section for this to cover not only academic awards but also business awards.

Our next section has to do with your special abilities as they apply to the position you are trying to land.

Skills and Qualifications

While not all resumes contain a skills section, this may be helpful when you want to emphasize the skills you have acquired from your various jobs or activities, rather than the duties, or the job title.

If you do not have enough previous experience for a specific job you are seeking for, it is important to emphasize your skills pertaining to that job.

Skills can be just as important as work experience to employers. To prepare this section you should:

- List jobs, activities, projects and special offices.
- Think of skills you have gained through those experiences.

- Group these skills into 3 - 5 job related skills categories and use these as headings.
- List your skills with significant details under the headings.
- Arrange headings in order of importance as they relate to your career objective.
- Arrange skills under headings in order of importance according to your goal.

In this section, you will also want to include any office machines you have experience operating, software programs you have become proficient in, and anything else that you feel might put you over the top with the job.

Example:
Leadership

- Conducted monthly club and board meetings for Lafayette Junior Woman's Club.
- Headed club's $8,000 philanthropic project sponsored by Tippecanoe County Historical Association.

- Coordinated responsibilities of committees to sell and serve food to 1500 people at fund raiser.

Business Communication

- Completed a formal report for Business Writing course.
- Wrote annual state and district reports of all club's community service projects, volunteered hours and monetary donations.
- Compiled, type, mimeographed and distributed club books to each member.

Financial Management

- Supervised the collection and dispersion of $4,000 in funds to various agencies and projects.
- Wrote and analyzed periodic business statements regarding funds to specific projects/agencies.

The next section can be worded in a couple of different ways. Here is where you want to let the potential employer know you have participated in activities and events as well as that you are a member of professional organizations along with any special awards that you have received.

A lot of this depends on whether or not you are fresh out of school looking for your first job or if you have been in the business world and are applying for another job.

Awards and Achievements

You can choose a few different ways to word this section. If you like, it can be titled "Activities and Honors" or "Awards and Organizations". It really is up to you. You have to tailor your resume to your specific needs as well as towards what type of job you are applying for.

This optional section points out your leadership, sociability and energy level as shown by your involvement in different activities. This should be your shortest section and should support your career objective. Additional information about activities can be included in your application letter or discussed at your interview.

You should:

- Select only activities and honors that support your career objective.
- List your college or professional organizations and arrange them in order of importance as they relate to your career objective.
- Include any office or official position you held.
- Spell out any acronyms your employer may not recognize.
- Include dates.

Example:

Accounting Club, President

Alpha Zeta Professional Fraternity

Purdue Grand Prix Foundation, President

Purdue Association for the Education of Young Children (PAEYC)

For any awards, you should include the year you received the award. You also may want to include a brief explanation of the criteria that you had to meet in order to get that honor.

Finally, you will wrap up your resume with a references section.

References

This is the shortest section of your resume because it should only consist of one sentence – "References are available upon request." You should generally not include references on your resume. You will put your references on a separate reference sheet, which we will address in the next section.

If the job you are applying for asks in the advertisement to include references when you send in your resume, you should change the "References" section to read "References are attached."

Which will makes a good transition into the next part of this book – your reference sheet.

4

References

You will want to have several different people on hand who will vouch for you as far as your character, your work habits, your work ethics, and your general value and worth as an employee and person.

You will want to have a minimum of three references and no more than five. At least one of these references should be a personal reference who is not a relative.

It can be a friend, a co-worker, or an acquaintance. The others should be work or school references.

The first rule of thumb for references is to ask the person first if you can use them as a reference when applying for jobs. As long as you have a good relationship with them, most people are happy to oblige for you and give you a glowing recommendation.

The purpose of a reference sheet is to have a list of people who can verify and elaborate on your professional experience for a potential employer. Past employers, professors, and advisors are the best professional references to have.

It is important to have a reference sheet because potential employers will often ask for a list of references they can contact.

If you included a statement such as "References Available upon Request" on your resume, you should be able to produce a reference sheet as soon as one is requested. In any case, having a reference sheet will save you time later on during the interview process.

Make sure to include people who know what type of person you are and who are familiar with your work. It is important to select individuals who know your distinctiveness so that they can provide a positive and accurate description of you to the employer or company in which you are seeking employment.

You should ALWAYS contact your references before including them on a reference sheet. It is also a good idea to give them a copy of your resume and talk to them about the job you are seeking so they will know how to best represent you.

When you are listing your references, you should include the following information:

- Your name
- Your present and permanent address (es)
- Your reference person or persons' information, which includes that person's:
    - Name
    - Department/Company
    - Title/Position
    - Address
    - Telephone number
    - Brief statement as to how you know this person.

It is not required to include the last part – the statement as to how you know this person, but it can help. That way if a potential employer does check your references, they know why you wanted to list them on your reference sheet.

Another very important part of the job application process is the cover letter that you will include with your resume.

5

The Cover Letter

The purpose of a cover letter is to introduce you and your resume as well as give some additional information about yourself to potential employers. You may also want to point out some parts of your resume you want the employer to pay special attention to.

An individually typed cover letter typically accompanies each resume you send out. Your cover letter may make the difference between obtaining a job interview and having your resume ignored. It makes sense to devote the necessary time and effort to write effective cover letters.

A cover letter should complement, not duplicate your resume. Its purpose is to interpret the data-oriented, factual resume and add a personal touch. A cover letter is often your earliest written contact with a potential employer, creating a critical first impression.

There are three different kinds of cover letters:

- The application letter responds to a specific job opening you have seen advertised
- The prospecting letter inquires about any job openings
- The networking letter which requests information and assistance in your job search

If you are sending out a resume, your application cover letter should always include a line in your cover letter that says where you found the advertisement for the job you are applying for. If you saw it in a newspaper, be sure to underline the name of the newspaper (grammar rules count!)

You should always tailor your cover letter to the specific job you are applying for. It's certainly easier to write generic or blanket cover letters than it is to write a cover letter specifically targeted to each position you apply for. However, if you don't invest the time in writing cover letters you're probably not going to get the interview, regardless of your qualifications.

Our first tip in writing a cover letter that works is to make a match between your qualifications and education with the job. This takes some time and effort and it's not always easy, but it's important. Take the job posting and list the criteria the employer is looking for.

Then list the skills and experience you have. Either address to how your skills match the job in paragraph form or list the criteria and your qualifications.

Do not design a form letter and send it to every potential employer (you know what you do with junk mail!).

Effective cover letters explain the reasons for your interest in the specific organization and identify your most relevant skills or experiences (remember, relevance is determined by the employer's self-interest). They should express a high level of interest and knowledge about the position.

To be effective, your cover letter should follow the basic format of a typical business letter and should address three general issues:

1. **First Paragraph** - Why you are writing

2. **Middle Paragraphs** - What you have to offer
3. **Concluding Paragraph** - How you will follow-up

In some cases, you may have been referred to a potential employer by a friend or acquaintance. Be sure to mention this mutual contact, by name, up front since it is likely to encourage your reader to keep reading!

If you are writing in response to a job posting, indicate where you learned of the position and the title of the position. More importantly, express your enthusiasm and the likely match between your credentials and the position's qualifications.

If you are writing a prospecting letter a letter in which you inquire about possible job openings - state your specific job objective. Since this type of letter is unsolicited, it is even more important to capture the reader's attention.

If you are writing a networking letter to approach an individual for information, make your request clear. The advantage to writing a letter like this and including your resume is that you will be making contacts in the business world and when a job opening comes up, they may still have your resume on file. It never hurts to be pro-active when looking for a job!

In responding to an advertisement, refer specifically to the qualifications listed and illustrate how your particular abilities and experiences relate to the position for which you are applying. In a prospecting letter express your potential to fulfill the employer's needs rather than focus on what the employer can offer you.

You can do this by giving evidence that you have researched the organization thoroughly and that you possess skills used within that organization.

Emphasize your achievements and problem-solving skills. Show how your education and work skills are transferable, and thus relevant, to the position for which you are applying.

Close by reiterating your interest in the job and letting the employer know how they can reach you and include your phone number and/or email address. If you want, you can make a bid directly for the job interview or informational interview and indicate that you will follow-up with a telephone call to set up an appointment at a mutually convenient time. Be sure to make the call within the time frame indicated.

In some instances, an employer may explicitly prohibit phone calls or you may be responding to a "blind want-ad" which precludes you from this follow-up. Unless this is the case, make your best effort to reach the organization. At the very least, you should confirm that your materials were received and that your application is complete.

If you are applying from outside the employer's geographic area you may want to indicate if you'll be in town during a certain time frame (this makes it easier for the employer to agree to meet with you).

In conclusion, you may indicate that your references are available on request. Also, if you have a portfolio or writing samples to support your qualifications, state their availability.

So, we've covered the three most important documents you need in a job search: the resume, the cover letter, and the reference sheet. Before you get excited and start mailing out your creations, there are some things that you need to do prior to that.

6

Making Sure You're Ready

You are trying to get a job and you are all ready with your resume, reference sheet, and cover letter. Before you get all excited and put your info in the mail, you will want to go through a few check points.

First and foremost, run a spell check on your computer. But don't stop there. Read your documents over and over to make sure there are no typographical or grammatical errors. It might also help to have someone else read over them as well to be sure that it looks the way it should.

The more people who see your resume, the more likely that misspelled words and awkward phrases will be seen (and corrected).

Here is a checklist to keep in mind for your cover letter:

- The contact name and company name are correct
- The letter is addressed to an individual, if possible
- The cover letter mentions the position you are applying for and where it was listed
- Your personal information is all included and correct

- If you have a contact at the company, mention him or her in the first paragraph of your cover letter
- The cover letter is targeted to the position you are applying for
- The letter is focused, concise, clear, and well organized
- If you have a gap in your employment history, explain it in your cover letter
- The font is easy to read
- No spelling or grammatical errors
- Read the cover letter out loud to make sure there are no missing words
- The cover letter is printed on good quality bond paper matching your resume
- You have kept a copy for yourself
- Your letter is signed

When it comes to your resume, there are also a few things to keep in mind. Much is the same as for the cover letter, but you want your resume to be tip top as well. Here's a checklist:

- There are no typographical or spelling errors
- The format is consistent throughout the entire document
- Use a good quality, heavier paper – heavier than regular copy paper
- You may want to use a colored paper, but make sure it is not garish like hot pink or neon green. Cream, gray, and off white are always good choices
- Use 8 ½" x 11" paper
- Print on only one side
- Use a font between 10 and 14 – you want it to be easy to read and look pleasant to the eye
- Use non-decorative fonts, but don't be afraid to experiment and use something a little interesting – just not TOO interesting!
- Stick to one font
- Avoid italics, scripts, and underlined words except for when underlining your headings
- Do not use horizontal or vertical lines, graphics, or shading.
- Do not fold or staple your resume.

- If you must mail your resume, put it in a large envelope and mail flat
- Be sure there is enough postage on the envelope to make it to the company
- When at all possible, deliver your resume in person and ask to speak with the personnel director when you do so.
- Follow up after a reasonable period of time if you have not heard anything. This shows initiative on your behalf and makes you memorable in the mind of the person doing the hiring.

Well, we've done a lot of talking about how to craft a resume and cover letter that gets attention. You probably want to see some sample of what we are talking about, don't you?

70

7

Resume Samples

There are literally hundreds of different ways you can write a resume and so many formats you can use, it can be mind-boggling. There are a lot of places on the Internet that can provide you with free templates that just require you to insert your personal information and then print it out. But feel free to use a few of these sample resumes that we like!

If you are applying for a creative job, it is all right to be creative with your resume, but not too creative. A professional position, however, necessitates a professional resume.

Whichever way you decide to go, be sure to have your resume be eye catching and intriguing. As we have said, the resume is your first introduction to your potential employer, so you will want to make the best first impression that you can right out of the gate.

Do some research and look for various formats that you can try with your own resume. There are many, many places on the Internet that offer up free templates where you can just fill in your own information and you are on your way.

We were able to find all sorts of places that offered up resume samples to use as guidelines to follow when you are typing up your own resume.

When you have a format to follow, it is much easier to make your resume – and you will be able to tailor the sample to fit your needs.

So, we offer up to you a few samples for you to consider when crafting a resume. Take them and use them as if they were your own.

CHLOE ZABATSKI

123 Alpha Street • Las Vegas, NV 12345 • (123) 555-1234 • chloez@bamboo.com

OBJECTIVE: Position as Personal Assistant / Office Manager

HIGHLIGHTS OF QUALIFICATIONS

- 15+ years experience providing outstanding administrative and personal support to a senior executive.
- A motivated self-starter, able to quickly grasp issues and attend to details while maintaining a view of the big picture. Expert in juggling multiple projects and achieving on-time completion within budget.
- Creative, resourceful and flexible, able to adapt to changing priorities and maintain a positive attitude and strong work ethic.
- A clear and logical communicator, able to establish rapport with both clients and colleagues, and motivate individuals to achieve organizational objectives.

PROFESSIONAL EXPERIENCE

1988-pres. **PERSONAL ASSISTANT & OFFICE MANAGER**
Paige & Associates, Denver, CO

Personal Assistant
- Provided continuous, high quality support to President/CEO. Coordinated schedule, appointments and travel arrangements; managed expense account and recovery.
- Proofed and edited speeches, reports and press releases; screened calls and communicated directives to Board members and company shareholders.
- Managed President's securities portfolio and prepared regulatory filings as needed. Acted as liaison to stockbrokers, accountants and legal counsel.
- Organized annual shareholder meetings, including site selection, catering and preparation of appropriate materials.
- Planned two major relocations: Assisted in site selection, worked with architect on interior design, and oversaw equipment/furniture/telecommunications setup without interruption in operations.

Office Manager
- Coordinated work flow among five consultants and supervised three support staff. Prioritized and delegated tasks, provided motivation and direction to create a positive work environment and ensured accurate, on-time completion.
- Tracked office expenses and created monthly reports for senior executive. Prepared invoices, Accounts Receivable/Payable and banking.
- Mediated conflicts among employees and between staff and management, utilizing diplomacy and humor to resolve issues.
- Responded to client needs and provided additional support where necessary.

Additional experience includes:
Seminar and Retreat Coordinator, Meditation, Inc., Reno, NV
On-site Massage Therapist, Reno Corporate Massage, Reno, NV

EDUCATION & TRAINING

B.A., Psychology, American University, Washington, DC
CMT / Somatic Educator, Somatic Institute, New York, NY
Additional training includes: Stress Management and Meditation

RANDI B. JENKINS
134 Whaler Cove • Port Washington, NY 12345 • 123-555-1234 • rbjenkins@bamboo.com

OBJECTIVE: Marketing or Marketing Management Position

HIGHLIGHTS OF QUALIFICATIONS
- May 2004 received M.B.A. Degree with emphasis in Marketing.
- Six years' experience in program development, international marketing, and Internet marketing.
- Highly effective leading and motivating teams to produce positive results while meeting deadlines.
- Strong communication, interpersonal, and presentation skills.

PROFESSIONAL MARKETING EXPERIENCE

COMTROTRON, New York, NY — 2003 to 2004
Marketing Consultant / Graduate Student Intern
- Interned as marketing consultant for this international e-business development company.
- Became integral team member in the development of online marketing programs for clients including AT&T, Avon, and Nike.
- Developed reports for clients including Avon's "Customer Needs and Reports Strategy."
- Conducted extensive research on the Internet, analyzed information, identified online solutions, and reported results to project leaders and clients.

COOKING TIME INTERNATIONAL PUBLICATIONS, New York, NY — 1998 to 2003
Publicity Manager
- Managed promotions and publicity campaigns for over 200 titles of international publishing company.
- Created promotional strategy, managed company website, and increased online promotions.
- Organized and conducted trade show presentations, promotional events, and seminars.
- On several occasions made guest appearances as a food expert for local network TV and radio stations.
- Made presentations on new directions and products at national and international cooking conferences.
- Supervised and trained staff of four including a publicist and marketing assistant.
- Pitched stories and secured placement in top 100 daily newspapers and high-profile magazines.
- Coordinated distribution of collateral such as catalogs, brochures, and point-of-sale materials.

LONDONMIST FRAGRANCES, London, England — 1997 to 1998
Assistant to Publicity Director / Student Intern
- Assisted in coordination of promotional campaign that launched EveningMist line product, "Shades."
- Maintained departmental records and correspondence; coordinated and scheduled meetings.

EDUCATION AND TECHNICAL SKILLS

M.B.A., Marketing, New York University, New York, NY — 2004

Relevant Coursework:
Relevant Coursework	Brand Management	Marketing Strategy	Sales Channel Mgt
Data Analysis	Sports & Events Mkg.	Global Management	Strategic Advantage
Leadership	Decision Modeling	Managerial Finance	Managerial Accounting

B.A., History, Adelphi College, Garden City, NY — 1997

Technical Skills - Illustrator, Photoshop, Filmaker, MS Access, Excel, PowerPoint, QuarkXpress

SARA FREMONT

5624 Oak Lane ~ St. Louis, Missouri 63031

314-555-1212 support@resumeedge.com

EDUCATOR
DRIVER & TRAFFIC SAFETY

Patient and caring Professional committed to helping students learn. Certified in driver and traffic safety from Midwest State University. Memberships include ADTSEA (American Driver Traffic Safety Education Association), MDTSEA (Midwest Driver Traffic Safety Education Association), and the National Association of Female Executives. Additional background as a Missouri Licensed Property Casualty Insurance Agent for Home, Auto, Health, and Life.

CERTIFICATION, LICENSURE, & EDUCATION

MIDWEST STATE UNIVERSITY, St. Louis, Missouri
Driver / Traffic Safety Education Certification, August 2002

~ Renewal of Missouri Educators License K-8, July 2002

MISSOURI EDUCATORS COLLEGE, St. Louis, Missouri
Graduate Level Coursework in Education, 1989-1990
G.P.A.: 3.83/4.00

Bachelor of Science Degree in Elementary Education, 1976
Semester Honors: 3.47/4.00   Semester Highest Honors: 4.00/4.00
Awarded compensated internship (for teaching)

PROFESSIONAL EXPERIENCE

FIRST CHOICE INSURANCE COMPANY, St. Louis, Missouri   April 1990 – July 2000
Insurance Agent
- Managed insurance agency daily operations, including territories and accounts.
- Fielded and resolved insurance sales questions; generated leads.
- Developed customer quotations and completed applications.
- Hired, trained, and motivated support personnel.
- Assessed client needs and established long-term client relationships.

Achievements:
   › Acknowledged as line leader of a four state territory for loss ratio, retention, and customer service.
   › Exceeded measured performance standards per ratios each of 10 years.

S&D RAILROAD COMPANY, St. Louis, Missouri   March 1979 – November 1987
Conductor
- Responsible for movement of freight traffic between pre-determined destinations.

Achievements
   › The first female to be employed by this train service.
   › Promoted from entry-level position within a very short period of time.

FRONTENAC SCHOOL DISTRICT, Frontenac, Missouri   October 1972 – March 1979
Transportation Department, Building & Grounds, and Substitute Teacher
- Employed during entire collegiate experience 20-40 hrs per week.

Dawn Toor

213.555.1212 ~ support@resumeedge.com

4431 Eastwick Village Drive ~ Charlotte, NC 11803

Artist

Award-winning Designer with degrees in Textiles and Oriental Painting. Background includes exhibiting work at the Manchester Gallery and successfully completing an internship with Ralston Technology in the United States. Fluent in English, Spanish, and Russian.

Awards & Exhibitions

- Third Place, LG Chemicals Design Contest, sponsored by LG Chemicals, Ltd., 1996
- Second Place, Textile Design Contest, sponsored by US Federation of Textile Industries, 1995
- Third Place, Noonan Design Contest, sponsored by the Noonan Company, 1995
- Third Place, US Modern Art Concours, 1994
- Five-time Recipient, Department Scholarship, 1992-1994

- Department of Textile Art Degree Exhibition, 1997
- Best Graduate Exhibition, Manchester Gallery, 1995
- Department of Oriental Painting Degree Exhibition, 1995
- Department of Oriental Painting Exhibition, 1994-1995
- US Modern Art Exhibition, 1994

Professional Experience

RALSTON TECHNOLOGY, INC., New York, USA 1999 – 2000
Intern, Art Department

- Successfully completed the presentation CD involving draping cars for Hyundai Motor Company of Korea.
- Concluded training for the Artworks Studio software GTxL cutter system.
- Traveled to Atlanta for the Bobbin Americas Expo from September 30 to October 2, 1999.

FIRST IMPORTS CHANNEL, CO., LTD., London, UK 1997 – 1998
Designer, Flooring Design Department

- Designed flooring products and conducted market research to determine client needs.
- Ensured quality of color matching by working closely with the manufacturer.

Education

WESTFALL UNIVERSITY, Bridgeport, Connecticut
Bachelor of Fine Arts, Department of Textile Art, 1997

NEW HAVEN COLLEGE, New Haven, Connecticut
Bachelor of Fine Arts, Department of Oriental Painting, 1995

SARA LIVINGSTON

1213 Flower ~ Beverly Hills, California 90210
800-555-1212 ~ support@resumeedge.com

OVERVIEW OF QUALIFICATIONS

- Award-winning, multi-lingual Interior Designer with an outstanding background in set design for NBC's *The Templetons*, TriStar's *Edge of Paradise*, and *Carrolton Returns* on PBS.
- High profile clientele includes Burt Williams, Trevor Sanders, Liz MacQuire, and R. Fredericks.
- Fluent in English, Spanish, Portuguese, German, and Italian; certified by the Design Institute of New York and Los Angeles; licensed designer in the United Kingdom, France, and Italy.

OUTSTANDING PROFESSIONAL ACCOMPLISHMENTS

- Chosen as *Designer of the Decade* in 1999 for work on *The Templetons* series.
- Received special Academy Award in 1992 for work on *Edge of Paradise*.
- Featured in *Vanity Fair*, *Time Magazine*, *Newsweek*, *Elle*, and *Interior Design*.
- Recognized as the youngest design entrepreneur with the launching of *Designs by Sara*.

EMPLOYMENT HISTORY

DESIGNS BY SARA, New York, Los Angeles, Rome, and London   1990 - 2001
Founder / President
- Established interior design / boutique catering to high net-worth clientele, including stars of stage, screen, and television.
- Oversaw daily operations, including purchasing, outsourcing, and client relations.
- Collaborated with online firm for *Designs by Sara* training course accredited by the Design Institute of New York and Los Angeles.
- Grew company from $.5 million in 1990 to $6 million annually in 1993.
- Recruited, trained, and directed activities of 17 design professionals.
- Launched satellite offices in Los Angeles in 1992, Rome in 1993, and London in 1994.
- Wrote weekly column in the *Los Angeles Times Magazine* on affordable interior design.
- Appeared on local newscasts with design tips.

COVENTRY INTERIORS, New York, New York   1989 - 1990
Intern
- Participated in client / designer meetings.
- Created design for firm's reception area that was chosen as best among 20 interns.
- Assisted junior designers with fabric, furniture, and accessory selection.

ACADEMIC BACKGROUND

DESIGN INSTITUTE OF NEW YORK, New York, New York
- Master of Arts in Interior Design, 1989
- Awarded the Francois Designation for Outstanding Interior Design Work, 1988-1989

DESIGN INSTITUTE OF LOS ANGELES, Los Angeles, California
- Bachelor of Arts in Interior Design, 1988

ASSOCIATIONS

- *Vice-President*, Interior Designers of America, 1999-Present
- *Member*, European Designers, 1997-Present

Tom Fitzgerald

6642 Overton Road
Portland, Oregon 97201
(503) 555-1212 ~ support@resumeedge.com

PROFILE
- Seasoned Professional with 20 years of experience in sales and sales management.
- Consistently awarded for outstanding performance; repeatedly won the *President's Club Award*, placing in the top 10% of company sales nationwide.
- Excels in public relations, marketing, human resources, and procedures administration.
- Licensed Real Estate Agent in the states of Oregon and California.
- Facilitates financial and business decisions for resort real estate companies.

EXPERIENCE

SALES MANAGEMENT
- Recruited, interviewed, hired, and trained all sales personnel.
- Managed all public relations, marketing, and sales for *Seasons Plus Resorts*, the largest vacation ownership company in the world.
- Developed an elite, goal-centered, cooperative sales force.
- Implemented and monitored productive property owner referral program.
- Directed site that was judged #1 within company in revenue per guest.

SALES
- Sold resort home sites as well as vacation properties to a marketed clientele.
- Won numerous awards as top performer and closer at all levels, including *President's Club Award* for sales in top 10% of the company nationwide.
- Directed building and sales of speculative property.
- Successfully completed sales leadership courses: "Dare to Soar" and "7 Habits of Highly Successful People."

ADMINISTRATION
- Grew company to $.5 million annual sales; broadened business scope from constructing small homes to developing high-end real estate properties.
- Bought property and oversaw home construction from start to finish.
- Hired all subcontractors and managed all payroll, insurance and taxes.

EMPLOYMENT

Director of Sales / Sales Manager, Seasons Plus Resorts, Portland, OR	2/99 – Present
Owner, Tom Fitzgerald Construction, Redding, California	6/90 – 12/98
Sales Professional, Seasons Plus Resorts, Portland, OR	6/85 – 5/90
Sales Professional, World Resorts, Portland, OR	4/82 – 5/85

EDUCATION

CIVIL ENGINEERING Western Tech, Portland, OR	9/76 – 5/78
BUSINESS California Community College, Redding, CA	9/75 – 5/76

8

Sample Cover Letters

As we've said, the cover letter can be just as important as the resume, so you will want it to look as professional and intriguing as it can. We found a few sample letters online that you may want to use to refer to when crafting your own cover letters.

7 Apple Court
Eugene, OR 97401
503-555-0303

Mr. Archie Weatherby
California Investments, Inc.
25 Sacramento Street
San Francisco, CA 94102

Dear Mr. Weatherby,

My outgoing personality, my sales experience, and my recently completed education make me a strong candidate for a position as an insurance broker for California Investments, Inc.

I recently graduated from the University of Oregon with a degree in marketing, where I was president of both the Future Business Leaders of America and the American Marketing Association.

Although a recent graduate, I am not a typical new graduate. I attended school in Michigan, Arizona, and Oregon. And I've put myself through these schools by working such jobs as radio advertising sales, newspaper subscription sales, and bartending, all of which enhanced my formal education.

I have the maturity, skills, and abilities to embark on a career in insurance brokering, and I'd like to do this in California, my home state.

I will be in California at the end of this month, and I'd like very much to talk with you concerning a position at California Investments. I will follow up this letter with a phone call to see if I can arrange a time to meet with you.

Thank you for your time and consideration.

Sincerely,

John Oakley

23 Hickory Tree Way
Belle Mead, NJ 08502
(908) 555-7495

September 12, 2006

Ms. Kristin Heller
The Research Institute
34 Marketing Court
Princeton, NJ 08540

Dear Ms. Heller,

As marketing companies are increasingly called upon to supply information on magazine readership to publishers, there is a growing need for trained and experienced professionals in the field.

Through my marketing/research experiences and my master's thesis, which have particularly dealt with improving marketing research studies so they can better define magazine audiences to potential advertisers, I am certain I could give you valuable assistance in satisfying research demands, managing key projects, and improving the marketing tools you currently use.

I will be completing my master's degree in December and would be interested in making a significant contribution to the Research Institute's profitability in a marketing/research capacity.

I am sure my services would be useful to you, and I will call you in early October to discuss an interview.

Thank you for your time and consideration.

Sincerely,

Scott Morris

1090 Peachtree Lane, #4
Atlanta, GA 30303
404/555-3030

Ms. Judy Sumner
Atlanta Board of Education
45 Peachtree Blvd.
Atlanta, GA 30303

Dear Ms. Sumner,

Perhaps I am the "multi-talented teacher" you seek in your "Multi-Talented Teacher" advertisement in today's Atlanta Constitution. I'm a versatile teacher, ready to substitute, if necessary, as early as next week. I have the solid teaching experience you specify as well as the strong computer skills you desire.

I am presently affiliated with a highly regarded private elementary school. Mr. Craig, the headmaster, will certainly give you a good reference. The details of your advertisement suggest to me that the position will involve many of the same responsibilities that I am currently performing.

In addition to the planning, administration, and student-parent counseling duties I highlight in my resume, please note that I have a master's degree as well as a teaching certificate from the state of Georgia.

> Knowing how frantic you must be without a fifth grade teacher, I will call you in a few days. Or if you agree upon reviewing my letter and resume that I am the teacher you need, call me at the home number listed above, or at 555-7327 during business hours.
>
> Thanking you most sincerely for your time and consideration.
>
> Cordially,
>
> Maria Plazza-Smith

These samples are more specific, but perhaps you would like some templates to work from. We were able to find some free cover letter templates online as well. Try a few of these on for size!

Your Name
Your Address
Your City, State, Zip Code
Your Phone Number
Your Email

Date

Name
Title
Organization
Address
City, State, Zip Code

Dear Mr./Ms. Last Name:

First Paragraph: Why You Are Writing. Remember to include the name of a mutual contact, if you have one. Be clear and concise regarding your request.

Middle Paragraphs: What You Have to Offer. Convince the readers that they should grant the interview or appointment you requested in the first paragraph. Make connections between your abilities and their needs or your need for information and their ability to provide it. Remember, you are interpreting your resume. Try to support each statement you make with a piece of evidence. Use several shorter paragraphs rather than one large block of text.

Final Paragraph: How You Will Follow Up. Remember, it is your responsibility to follow-up; this relates to your job search. State that you will do so and provide the professional courtesy of indicating when (one week's time is typical). You may want to reduce the time between sending out your resume and follow up if you fax or e-mail it.

                                              Sincerely,

                                         Your Signature

                                         Your Typed Name

Your Name
Your Address
Your City, State, Zip Code
Your Phone Number
Your Email

Date

Name
Title
Organization
Address
City, State, Zip Code

Dear Mr./Ms. Last Name:

Your Requirements:

- Responsible for evening operations in Student Center and other facilities, including managing registration, solving customer problems, dealing with risk management and emergencies, enforcement of department policies.
- Assists with hiring, training, and management of staff. Coordinate statistics and inventory.
- Experience in the supervision of student staff and strong interpersonal skills are also preferred.
- Valid Minnesota driver's license with good driving record. Ability to travel to different sites required.
- Experience in collegiate programming and management.

My Qualifications:

- Register students for courses, design and manage program software, solve customer problems, enforce department policies, and serve as a contact for students, faculty, and staff.
- Hiring, training, scheduling and management of staff, managing supply inventory, and ordering.
- Minnesota driver's license with NTSA defensive driving certification.
- Extensive experience in collegiate programming and management.
- Excellent interpersonal and communication skills.

I appreciate your taking the time to review my credentials and experience. Again, thank you for your consideration.
Sincerely,

Your Signature

Your Typed Name

Your name
Mailing address
City, state, and zip
Telephone number(s)
Email address
Today's date

Your addressee's name
Professional title
Organization name
Mailing address
City, state and zip

Dear Mr. (or Ms.) last name,

Start your letter with a grabber—a statement that establishes a connection with your reader, a probing question, or a quotable quote. Briefly say what job you are applying for.

The mid-section of your letter should be one or two short paragraphs that make relevant points about your qualifications. You should not summarize your resume! You may incorporate a column or bullet point format here.

Your last paragraph should initiate action by explaining what you will do next (e.g., call the employer) or instigate the reader to contact you to set up an interview. Close by saying "thank you."

Sincerely yours,
Your handwritten signature
Your name (typed)

Your Name
Your Address
Your City, State, Zip Code
Your Phone Number
Your Email Address

Date

Employer Contact Information
Name
Title
Company
Address
City, State, Zip Code
Salutation

Dear Mr./Ms.

Body of Cover Letter

The body of your cover letter lets the employer know what position you are applying for, why the employer should select you for an interview, and how you will follow-up.

First Paragraph:

The first paragraph of your letter should include information on why you are writing. Mention the position you are applying for. Include the name of a mutual contact, if you have one. Be clear and concise regarding your request.

Middle Paragraphs:

The next section of your cover letter should describe what you have to offer the employer. Convince the reader that they should grant the interview or appointment you requested in the first paragraph. Make strong connections between your abilities and their needs. Mention specifically how your skills and experience match the job you are applying for. Remember, you are interpreting your resume, not repeating it. Try to support each statement you make with a piece of evidence. Use several shorter paragraphs or bullets rather than one large block of text.

Final Paragraph:

Conclude your cover letter by thanking the employer for considering you for the position. Include information on how you will follow-up. State that you will do so and indicate when (one week's time is typical). You may want to reduce the time between sending out your resume and follow up if you fax or e-mail it.

Complimentary Close:

Respectfully yours,

Signature:

Handwritten Signature (for a mailed letter)

Typed Signature

9

Sample Reference Sheets

Your reference sheet is important to have as well – like we stated earlier. While this will not be mailed along with your resume and cover letter, you will still need to have it on hand during an interview so that you can produce it when your potential employer asks for it.

Here are some sample reference sheets for you when creating your own reference sheet.

Here are some sample reference sheets for you when creating your own reference sheet.

CARRIE E. COMPLETE

PRESENT ADDRESS
123 Hawkins Graduate House
West Lafayette, IN 47906
(317) 555-1123

PERMANENT ADDRESS
12334 N. College Avenue
Indianapolis, IN 46220
(317) 555-1829

REFERENCES

Professor John English
Sociology Department
Purdue University
Stone Hall
West Lafayette, IN 47907
(317) 555-6000

Professor English is my academic advisor and is presently supervising my research in an independent study sociology course.

Mrs. Diana Handie
Food Services Supervisor
Hawkins Graduate House
Purdue University
West Lafayette, IN 47907
(317) 555-2323

Mrs. Handie was my supervisor when I worked in the Hawkins Cafeteria.

Mrs. Jennifer Active
Activity Therapy Staff Wabash Valley Mental Health Center

2900 North River Road
West Lafayette, IN 47906
(317) 564-9600

Mrs. Active is my current employer.

References for James Esterman

433 Colby Hall
Hutchinson University
Hutchinson, IL 60353
(847-555-2733)
esterj01@hutch.edu

Dr. Pat Wombat
Professor of Psychology
Hutchinson University
Hutchinson, IL 60353
wombatp@hutch.edu
(847-555-3212)

Dr. Wombat was my supervisor in
the Human Subjects Research Lab.

Dr. Chris Murphy
Professor of Biology
Hutchinson University
Hutchinson, IL 60353
(847-555-2733)

Dr. Murphy was my professor in
Biology 425: Special Research Projects.

Mr. Michael McCollins
Project Director
The Acme Corporation
112221 Main Street
Hutchinson, IL 60353
(847-555-2813)

Mr. Murphy supervised my internship
at the Acme Corporation.

Ms. Sonia Ramirez
Manager
The Rasmussen Corporation
1192 Elston Avenue
Chicago, IL 60105
(312-555-2733)
SRamirez@rasmussen.com

Ms. Ramirez supervised my co-op
experience at the Rasmussen Corporation.

IM A SAMPLE
1234 North 55 Street
Bellevue, Nebraska 68005
(402) 292-2345
iasample@aol.com

PROFESSIONAL REFERENCES

Name
Position
Title
Company
Address City, State, Zip Code
Company Phone Number

(Examples)
Bernard E. Langer
Director, Human Resources
Attaboy Company
7833 Avenue G
Omaha, NE 68134
(402) 738-4467

Dr. Sandra P. Doolittle
Chemistry Professor
Bellevue University
1000 Galvin Road South
Bellevue, NE 68005
(402) 293-5543

Gregory J. Throckmortan (Former Supervisor)
General Manager
Iowa Western Beef Company
234 6th Avenue
Council Bluffs, IA 51510
(712) 355-7865

So you have your resume out there and you got the phone call for an interview. This next section will be brief, but there are some things to keep in mind when you are face to face with a prospective employer during a job interview. Hopefully, our advice will help you get the job!

10

The Interview

The first thing that you want to remember when you are at a job interview is that first impressions count. Dress appropriately for the job. No matter what, though, never wear jeans to a job interview – it doesn't matter how casual the job is that you are applying for, jeans are inappropriate in any situation.

For women, a nice skirt and dress or a suit is what you should wear. For men, a suit is most appropriate, but you can get away with a pair of khaki pants and a nice polo shirt.

When you are talking to your interviewer, be enthusiastic about the job. Convey your excitement about the possibility of working for this company and always, always smile.

If you are applying for a creative position or a teaching position, you might want to bring along a portfolio of your work so that you can show off your creativity. Having samples of what you can do can make you stand out over other applicants.

Above everything else, be excited and enthusiastic about your possible job. When you are happy about being there, it will show in your demeanor and your responses. We can't stress enough how much this can make a difference in getting the job and not getting the job.

Your job interview is when you get the chance to shine. Be sure and answer all of the questions accurately and with enthusiasm. Try not to hesitate and be prepared for anything. This writer once had an interview for a sales position where the interviewer asked me to sell him a pen. I was able to think on my feet and gave him a great sales pitch. I got the job!

You can be just as successful as I was when you take the time to be prepared for your interview and then shine during the talk you are having with the person doing the hiring. It is truly your personality that will get you the job along with your experience and your education.

Once you get the interview, it is all up to you, but you can do it. The person interviewing you already knows a lot about you from your perfectly crafted resume that we have taught you how to put together.

Conclusion

When you are looking for a job, having the right tools at your disposal is extremely important. Those tools include having a killer resume along with a compelling cover letter that will help prospective employers choose you over anyone else.

We have given you a lot of advice about how to craft your resume to put your best foot forward to make you look great for the job and compel them to call you first over any other applicant. What you need to do is stand out over the competition and be sure that you are the one that gets the interview!

There is a lot that goes into making a resume that works. When you have all of the basic components in place, you can make a resume that works for you and one that will help you get a job. And, after all, that is your end result, now isn't it?

Take your time making your resume and be sure that it reflects who you are and what you can do. Let your resume speak for you and your abilities and be sure to follow up on all of the places you have submitted your resume to.

We hope that you are able to get your dream job with the advice we have given. But remember that a lot of the most important parts have to do with you!

Good luck and happy job searching!

I hope this was a pleasant read ☺

Warmest Regards

CPSIA information can be obtained
at www.ICGtesting.com
Printed in the USA
LVOW12s1613231216
518584LV00003B/497/P